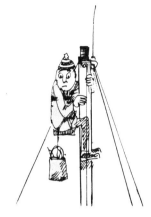

# imminent all areas

# imminent all areas

**Mike Peyton**

NAUTICAL

First published in Great Britain by
**Nautical Books** an imprint of **A & C Black Ltd**

ISBN 0 7136 5720 0

Printed in Great Britain by
Butler & Tanner Ltd, Frome and London

To Danny

Many of these cartoons first appeared
in either *Yachts and Yachting* or
*Practical Boat Owner*.

# Contents

# 1  Dry ships

*'You don't think we should wait a fortnight?'*

'He's flying "K" Sir – I wish to communicate with you!'

'Yes I did say blisters – here, on my hand.'

'Look theres the Maynards'

'John, you must be out of your tiny mind, come down at once!'

*'Do you subscribe to this theory that it's a status symbol?'*

'I'll make you a straight swap – here and now.'

'I'll give you a hand – what wants doing?'

'All I'm saying is it will have to be a damn good holiday.'

'The children have never enjoyed a holiday like this one.'

# 2 Slightly offshore

'If you tell me it's not like this in "Howard's Way" again, I'll do you.'

'She's best on a run.'

'I appreciate it's none of our business sir, but it could be.'

'Relax, he's on a board not a bank.'

*'Bit different from the brochure – Cruise the sunny East coast in a yacht of character.'*

'I'll see you later. I made a promise out there – I'm going to church.'

'Do you ever think that there may be pleasanter ways of spending the weekends?'

'Quiet Essex creek my foot, the quicker I get home for some sleep the better.'

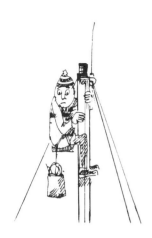

# 3 Ups and Downs

'The feeling I get at the Boat Show is that boats like this don't exist and weather like this never happens.'

'What do you mean exhilarating? Only twenty minutes ago you gave me the boat – and I told you where you could stuff it!'

*'OK, drop the staysail.'*

'I've got most of it away.'

'I could have sworn I saw a windsurfer.'

'Would you ask John to go to Channel 77 so I could have a word with him?'

'Well the least you can do is take a line ashore with you!'

*'Coastguard on the radio wanting name and address of your next of kin.'*

# 4  Handicapped

*'I've been on these long tacks before.'*

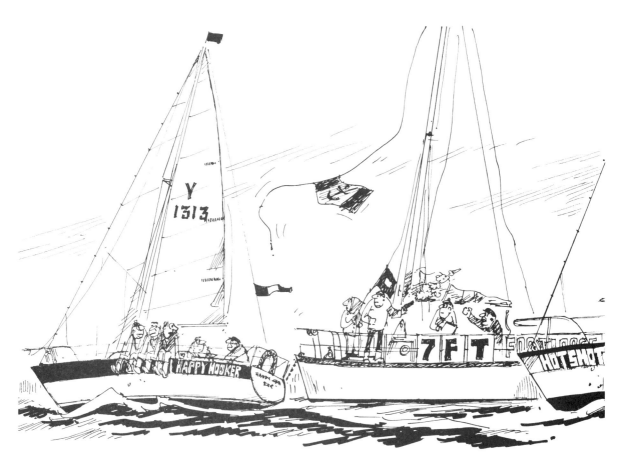

'A good start admitted, but I think the Committee Boat will protest.'

'It beats me what they see in a boat like that.'

'Have you ever stopped to analyse what we're doing?'

'Don't lean on the mast, mate, you'll have it down.'

'Just keep going, the ones on port will smile and say thank you and the ones on starboard will call you an ignorant bast...'

'It beats me why we're always the backmarker.'

# 5  Between Brest and the Elbe

'Relax! I've got a backbearing that clears everything.'

*'Is it supposed to remind you of an egg cup ... keep to the East, or a wine glass ... keep to the West?'*

'What do you mean go outside and have a look? I'm not short sighted.'

*'I'm not doubting you dear but are you sure we have a fair tide?'*

PEYTON

'It's getting a bit fraught George, we've run out of gin.'

'I stop being a purist at Force Five.'

*Le chasseur de pavillons.*

*'You don't have to tell me we've got a problem, just turn the shaft slowly
in reverse.'*

'I suppose it's fair to say that we have a chance.'

'According to an article I read, the reason you're feeling nausogenic is because the sinusoidal vertical oscillation is exactly on a frequency of 0.19 hertz.'

'Did you catch the forecast?'

*'Ease her down Joe, I've lost the leading marks.'*

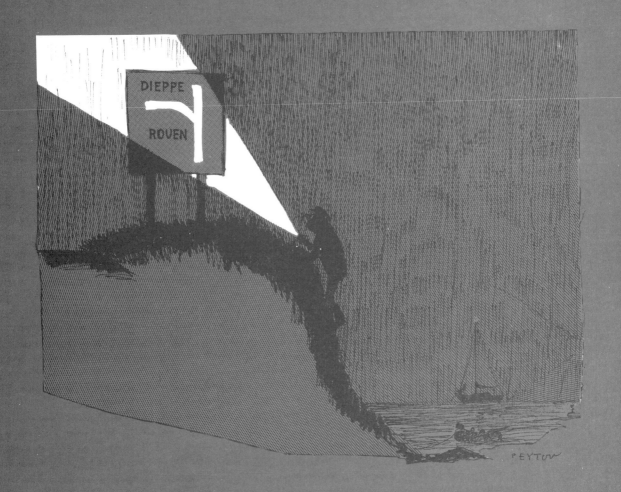

DIEPPE

ROUEN

PEYTON

# 6   A snug berth

*'No, she hasn't come out of her berth . . . but . . .'*

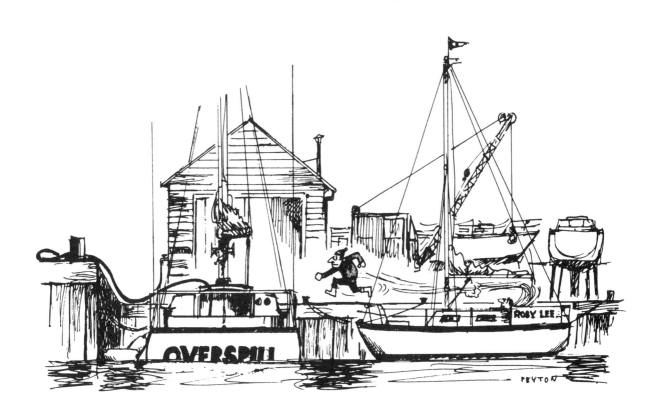

'Sorry I missed it too, I dozed off between 'Danny Boy' and 'Men of Harlech'.

'Blokes at the office think it's a floating love nest I bring birds to.'

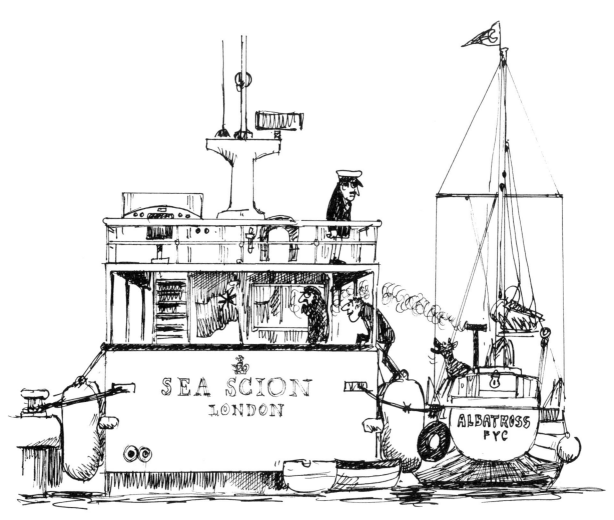

*'I thought you yotties were all matey like, brotherhood of the sea and all that.'*

*'She came in a few hours ago. They're in the Jolly Sailor if you want them.'*

'Excuse me miss but would you tell Mr Benson his wife has reported him overdue and there's a full scale search and rescue operation for him.'

'*I know, I know, you've got to put sailcovers on because polyester deteriorates in sunshine.*'

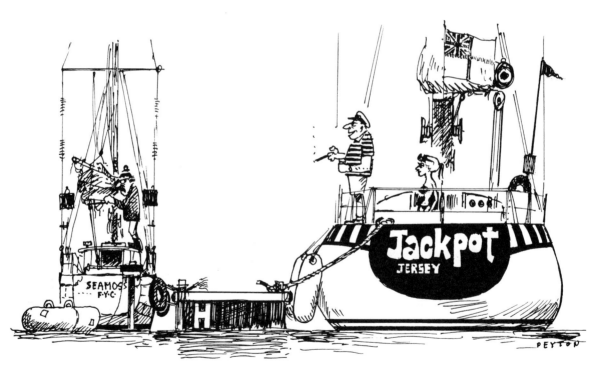

'Lot of fun to be had with a boat like that, had one myself years ago.'

'What narks me is we're paying to do it.'

'Doesn't look as if "Deversoir" is back.'

*'The trouble with these outdoor shows is that they're too much like the real thing.'*

'We can stop at Mothers on the way home.'

# 7 Back at the yard

'It's lucky we came down to check.'

'It's your mother-in-law Mr Miller. She thought you might be interested – your wife's had twins.'

*'That man who told you not to park there – stupid fool you called him – was the crane driver and he's gone home early.'*

'There are some thoughtless fools about.'

*'There's something about these old traditional yar...'*

*'Well it seems fair enough to me. Last Christmas we spent at your mother's. This Christmas . . .'*

'I've noticed it after every boat show, a certain discontent with their lot.'

'...and just dump it – don't come back with anything else that might come in handy.'

# 8 Home Waters

'I've passed! I'm a Yachtmaster!'

'Hello Darling!!! I'm b . a . . c . . . k . . . .'

'Why is Daddy going back to the boat? – well he could have forgotten to turn off the seacock on the toilet, or the water inlet on the engine, or the master switch on the electrics or the greaser on the stern gland or the gas bott . . .'

*'I forgot to mention dear, I put some sails in the bath to soak.'*

'We're doing all we can skipper, in the meantime I'll just hand you over . . .'

'No I'm not busy John, I'll grab my oilskins and see you at the marina in twenty minutes.'